REVIEW OF MY CAT

TANNER RINGERUD | JACK SHEPHERD

 sourcebooks

Published by Sourcebooks, Inc.
P.O. Box 4410, Naperville, Illinois 60567-4410
(630) 961-3900
Fax: (630) 961-2168
www.sourcebooks.com

Library of Congress Cataloging-in-Publication data is on file with the publisher.

Printed and bound in China
OGP 10 9 8 7 6 5 4 3 2 1

-ACKNOWLEDGMENTS-

Thanks to Eric Karjala for the first-ever cat review; to Bull, Meg, and Princess Cuteyface for tolerating us; and to anyone who ever woke up one day and thought, "You know, I think today is the day on which I will review my cat."

-INTRODUCTION-

Let's face it—cats aren't always *perfect*. I mean, whatever, let's walk that back a bit—cats are better than dogs, and they're better than most people, and they clearly live out their lives in a sublime state of total enlightenment on an exalted plane of existence that transcends petty human concerns like "making a living," or "helping around the house," or even "thinking about things." But they're not always *perfect*. That's all.

Unfortunately, up until very recently, there was no way for anyone to know this, because, due to a massive oversight (for which someone in charge was hopefully severely punished), there was no system in place for reviewing or ranking these animals with whom we share our lives and who we love unconditionally and who sit on our laptops. And it is well-known in philosophy that if you can't assign numbers to a thing on some website in order to determine its value to you, then, well, you barely even know which way is up with that thing! I am pretty sure this is a thing in philosophy.

What were we talking about? Oh yeah! Think about it: Restaurant-goers have Yelp; movie lovers have Rotten Tomatoes; tourists have the Michelin Guide; even dog lovers are able to go outside and talk to each other in real life. But up until recently there was NOTHING for cats. No way to rank them! No review of cats. It makes me angry just thinking about it!

Well, now there is an official way to review your cat. That's what we've been leading up to. In the last year, thousands of cat owners have looked deep inside their souls and taken off their rose-tinted glasses and really *scrutinized* their cats from an objective point of view for probably the first time in the history of the cat-human partnership. And the results have been really interesting.

What we're talking about here is nothing less than *official*, *objective* reviews by real cat owners of their previously unexamined, unaccountable feline roommates. And we know that these reviews are official, because they are all composed according to the four major criteria for cat excellence that are accepted by every sanctioned Cat Review Committee in the world: Appearance, Sociability, Usefulness, and Huggability. But this is the truly crazy part: In a development that shocked the entire cat community, not everyone got a perfect score. Cats aren't always perfect, it turns out.

OK, let's get to some reviews. Try not to judge these cats too harshly. A few of them vaguely mean well.

-THE GOOD-

Human beings have been fighting for years to get to the top of the food chain. We're adapted to be bigger, stronger, and smarter than almost every other being on the planet. Our bodies and minds have become highly specialized. It's theorized that our distant ancestors were only about three and a half feet tall, and it's incredible to think about how far we've come. But there's still one species that dominates us—cats.

Cats have gone the opposite direction over the past few generations. What were once massive, powerful killing machines are now docile ornaments. They just lie around in whatever spot of sunshine they can find, waiting for us to fawn over them and feed them. It's actually a pretty brilliant move on their part. They've adapted in every way to be our masters. They control everything we do.

Think about it. How many other species out there have so much control over us? Dogs maybe? Dogs don't count. They appreciate it too much. They're way too eager. It's gauche. It's nowhere near the same dynamic we have with cats. We feed them, we seek their affection, and we get rid of their poop for them. And for all that, what do we get back? It depends on who you ask. A lot of people would say *nothing*. But cat moms and cat dads know better.

It's the little things that make it all worthwhile. A gentle head butt on our shins when we get home, an evening spent quietly curled up in our laps, the way they come looking for affection when we're sitting on the toilet. Cats don't care. They may be small moments, but they mean so much to all of us. Our cats make it clear that despite everything, they love us. That's why we do it. That's why we love them.

Sure, they may have evolved their way out of being the dominant species on the planet. They may be small and harmless, but despite that, cats don't need us. No, we need them. And luckily, they oblige. They grace us with their divine presence. This section is dedicated to those cats. The cats that all other cats—no, all living creatures—should aspire to be like.

Lil Bub

Owner: Mike

Appearance: A

BUB has physical attributes that trump those of common Earth cats. Her giant green eyes penetrate the deepest reaches of your soul. She looks so amazing that it feels wrong to even give her appearance a letter grade. She should get a crown or a throne instead. Or just a giant fish. Can you guys give her a giant fish?

Sociability: A

BUB is a space cat, and for some reason she loves humans. She will voluntarily clean your beard, your arm, or your nose at any given moment. She will sleep for hours curled up on your lap or on your chest and can magically heal your bones and cure your anxiety with the subsonic harmonics of her astonishingly loud, rumbling purr.

Usefulness: A

BUB has helped save the lives of thousands of pets around the planet. Also, she is currently working on saving the planet itself.

Huggability: A

You can literally hug BUB for eternity, if you were incredibly patient and immortal like her. She is like a living stuffed animal— from space.

grade: (A+)

Zulie

Owner: Frann

Usefulness: A

As useful as a cat can be. No danger of oversleeping with the alarm cat around. Kills bugs dead. Hours of entertainment and lap warming. Has not yet mastered washing dishes or calculating taxes, but the shortage of opposable thumbs and neocortical brain matter are disabilities for which we make reasonable accommodation.

Huggability: A

See above regarding lap warming. Tolerates the sudden "scoop and snuggle" with good grace, possibly in hopes of better access to tuna treats.

grade: A

Good job!

Zoobilee Zoo

(aka Zooey)

Owner: Julia

Huggability: A

Basically, Zooey wants me to get a BabyBjörn to carry him around in. He wants to be held and carried 100 percent of the time. His favorite is to be carried around like a baby with his face close to my face. It's to the point where if I crouch down to get something out of the fridge, he'll come over and put his front paws on my shoulders and try to climb on board. He's big on hugging.

grade:

Leonard

Owner: Adam

Appearance: A

Visitors to his home (and mine) always comment on his cute face, which has some delightfully elegant racing-stripe patterns and long, striking whiskers.

Sociability: A

Leonard likes to give you a "cat hug," where he gets in a position in which he is straddling you belly to belly and purrs very loudly. It's a very nice experience, especially when you have a case of the icks.

Usefulness: B

He learned his trade on the mean streets of Crown Heights, Brooklyn, which means that he's a great mouser and that he has an appetite for Italian American food like baked ziti, lasagna, and pizza. He begs like a madman for anything with sauce and cheese.

Huggability: A

Just look at the picture and you will immediately want to hug this cute cat-boy. When he gets super tired and relaxed, he will fall asleep with his tongue sticking out. Now how would you not want to hug such a sweet, lovely being!

grade: A-

Agatha

Owners: Dan and Annie

Appearance: A+

Agatha's beauty is so surreal—she's like an artist's interpretation of the perfect cat combined with the adorable nature of a Pokémon. She's also a third the size of a normal adult cat. We feel her miniature stature actually makes her an A+.

Sociability: A

Agatha loves to meet new people and touch their food.

grade: (A)

Parsley

Owner: Harrie

Appearance: C

For an eighteen-year-old, Parsley is pretty good-looking, working hard to maintain her youthful looks by taking regular naps and avoiding too much strain. Her fur is as soft as always, and she is quite skinny. But at least she's not at risk of developing cankles.

Sociability: A

Parsley loves company—so much so that she often (accidentally) gets trodden on while making attempts to gain our attention. She often has male pursuers popping through the cat flap, and we imagine she puts out, although she has had the snip, so sadly no mini-Parsleys.

Usefulness: F

She mostly gets in the way—and dribbles a fair bit. But you can forgive her for it.

grade: **B—**

Upgraded from a C— by the editors because she seems like such a lovely old girl.

Aphrodite

Owner: Bri

Appearance: A

Aphrodite appears to be more of a majestic lioness, rather than your ordinary house cat. She has big eyes that are slightly slanted, which makes her look a bit sexy. Her hair is long and luscious, and very well kept. She's definitely eye candy for the other nonmajestic male felines—and "they be lining down the block just to watch what she got," as it were.

Usefulness: B

Aphrodite is useful about once a month. When she isn't spending her days bouncing around the house like a lunatic that has just been freed from a psych ward or prancing around like she's the queen of England, she'll catch a mouse and bring it to my room and show me what a good job she's done.

grade: B+

Carson

Owner: Mallory

Appearance: A

Carson is most definitely a lady-killer. His silky black fur that he spends 75 percent of the day grooming is oh, so soft and velvety. This, combined with his heavy eyelids and his abnormally long canines, make him akin to Edward from the *Twilight* saga, and he has no less of an effect on the females that grace his presence.

Sociability: B

Carson doesn't understand unspoken cat boundaries and will rush up to any new feline he sees, which usually results in a swift slap and hiss from the offended.

Usefulness: C

Carson isn't useful in helping fold laundry, pay bills, or clean up after himself, but he is useful if you want a loud, genuine purr or forehead kisses in the morning, or to be unconditionally loved by a furry little man.

Huggability: D

Who needs hugs when you can have snacks? Pretty sure that's Carson's motto.

grade: C+

Buster

Owner: Kelly

Appearance: A

Buster knows how to use his looks to his advantage and work the camera. I often wonder what it would be like to be a stage mom for a cat model.

Sociability: C

He has a penchant for chasing (and getting a little too rough with) his sister, Lyla. But other than that, he plays hard to get. Maybe his looks have gone straight to his cat brain.

Usefulness: C

What Buster lacks in usefulness, he makes up for by throwing one cute cat glance my way to melt my heart. "Of course I will get off of the couch during a pivotal scene of this critically acclaimed drama to turn on the water on the other side of the apartment for you, Buster."

Wait, is he manipulating me?

grade: C+

Noah

Owners: Matt and Lou

<u>Usefulness: A</u>

If his job is to be entertained and play, then Noah gets an A. He will chase people around like a dog would (in fact, it's his favorite thing to do). And he likes to plop onto hard surfaces (like kitchen floors) and be spun around really, really fast. He's also very strange and frequently bolts across the house at warp speed for no reason, which is highly entertaining. Noah may not do the dishes or take out the trash, but he's very useful when it comes to providing a laugh or smile.

grade:

Josie

Owner: Jason

Sociability: A

Josie is quite the conversationalist. She will converse on a wide variety of subjects and loves interjecting her thoughts in the middle of a group conversation. Her means of conveying these thoughts can range from a simple "Ma!" to the more delicate "Mooow?" to the more pronounced "Mooooooowowowooooow." However, Josie has limits. When these limits are violated, Josie expresses herself by saying "Noooooo!"

Huggability: B

Josie can be hugged and loved on for long periods of time as long as you're willing to listen to her tell you exactly how she feels about it. And she will tell you exactly how she feels about it.

Puck

(aka Dr. Puck and The Doctor)

Owner: Victoria

Usefulness: D

Generally pretty useless. Sleeps, eats, looks out the window, and tries to eat bugs. Unless you need help gathering Q-tips or bobby pins (which he somehow finds and stores in his water bowl), he is not a helpful roommate.

Huggability: A

When you are standing and doing chores, Puck wants to be part of the experience and insists that you hold him. He does this by putting his front paws on your legs and looking up at you desperately, as if he would die of sorrow if you didn't hold him while cleaning the kitchen.

grade: C

Food

Malachy

*(aka Mister Cat, Fluffaman,
or Special Fluffababyman)*

Owner: B.

Appearance: A

- ☆ Soft, extremely fluffy
- ☆ Excellent whisker length
- ☆ Pleasing toe beans
- ☆ The top few inches of his tail are bent from the rest of it and flick around when he's interested in something, which is super charming
- ☆ More than a few houseguests have exclaimed over his beauty—he is just that fetching

Usefulness: B

Points off for vomiting more than seems necessary and for figuring out the best way to annoy me into wakefulness at 7 a.m. A MILLION POINTS TO FLUFFINDOR for providing a really significant source of calm and comfort in my anxiety-prone life.

Huggability: C

HE IS A SWEET, FLUFFY GENTLEMAN AND I ADORE HIM.

grade:

Java

Owners: Caitlin and Chad

Sociability: B

Java is very social with my boyfriend and me. She loves to play and has even made herself a wonderful new toy out of our dog's "cone of shame."

Usefulness: A

We adopted Java for our two-year-old black lab, Flynn, who has separation anxiety. It sounds odd, but they seem to really love each other's company and are like each other's own personal shadows. Java's usefulness has been met!

grade: B+

Ted

Owner: Willy

Sociability: B

Ted is most definitely a lover, not a fighter. Rarely known to hiss. He even takes the occasional stroll with the ginger girl next door! What a ladies' man.

Huggability: A

If one thing can be said about Ted, it's that he loves to be held. On his back like a baby, slung over a shoulder, or sprawled out over your chest, Ted loves it. He likes belly rubs, chin scratches, and just general love.

grade:

Frankie

Owner: Emily

Sociability: A

Frankie will meow at you at the mention of his name. He comes when he is called and loves being a lap cat.

Huggability: A

Frankie takes every hug like a champion, and even the occasional toss around from children. He usually takes whatever he can get, and so is ultimately the most literal cat version of "taking one for the team."

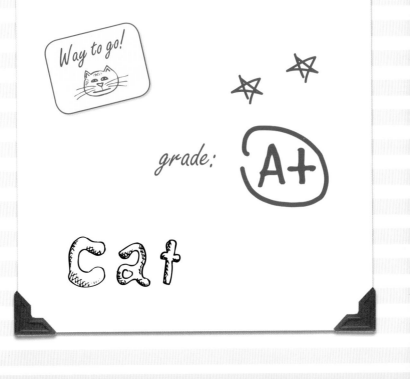

Way to go!

grade: A+

cat

Gatsby

Owner: Megan

Appearance: A

Gatsby has an extra-long tail to help him with his jumping, which he just realized he could do, and little blue eyes. Rarely seen, since he's asleep most of the time.

Sociability: A

Gatsby loves playing. He loves playing with the people of the house, the puppy, and the other cat. He loves when you throw his toy mice, because he'll bring them back so he can go fetch them again. He also likes hiding under the sheets when we make the bed so he can attack our hands.

Usefulness: B

Gatsby puts his toys in his toy basket and pulls them out when he wants to play. Downside: He doesn't contribute to the rent.

Huggability: A

He's always down for playtime. He's always there for a good laugh. He's always down to cuddle, no matter who you are. Whenever this little guy is around, you're guaranteed some sort of enjoyment.

grade: A-

Sammy

(aka Winchester)

Owner: Megan

Appearance: A

Sammy is an orange short-haired tabby with a white, furry (and fat) belly. WOMEN LOVE HIM.

Usefulness: B

Other than the comforting rubbing of his head under your chin and the playful stalking, he is pretty much just a lazy fatty who sleeps most of the day.

Huggability: A

He loves hugs! Just not when he's busy catching a lizard.

grade: A-

Frenchetta
(more often Angel Cat)

Owners: Michelle and Christian

Huggability: A

Frenchetta is so huggable that she tolerates bath time because she likes the aftermath where we wrap her in a towel and snuggle her in bed. She also lets a few select humans drape her around their neck like a slain deer.

grade: A

Falcon Jeffers Rajt

Owner: Lindsay

Appearance: A

Falcon is very handsome. With pink toe pads, a pale pink nose, and Neapolitan ears, he is hard to resist. Also he has a cotton tail and a soft while belly like a baby bunny.

Sociability: B

Falcon is complicated. The shelter described him as a "private investigator"—he's initially standoffish and suspicious, but once he gets to know you, he loves to be held like the football in a Heisman Trophy, he enjoys drooling all over you, and he will gladly accept chin, belly, or ear scratches.

Usefulness: A

Falcon really excels in this category. Whether it is capturing a bug or a toy, or alerting you to danger, he is priceless. He is a skilled jumper, and he's the only cat I've ever seen capable of doing a pull-up.

Huggability: A

All day long.

grade: **A**

Desi

Owner: Matt

Appearance: A+

Desi is the most beautiful cat in the world. I'm tempted to say, "Desi is the most beautiful woman in the world," but the consensus is that that's creepy.

Usefulness: B+

Desi is a bit uncoordinated and often falls off of things or tries unsuccessfully to jump on furniture. This has significant comic value (I'm pretty sure that's why she does it). She also has the deepest, loudest, rumbliest purr ever. When she lies on your chest, the sound and vibration are very soothing and aid in digestion and sleep. Also, there's the companion thing.

grade:

Good job!

Our best cat. The best cat. Better than your cat.

Pudding

Owner: Amy

Appearance: A

I think he's a beautiful boy, so I give him an A on that one. Just look at that picture of him sniffing flowers.

Sociability: C

I'd give him a C here because he's not a real social cat. He's very laid back: "you stay in your space, I'll stay in mine." Normally, I get the snuggly type cats, but he is not at all snuggly.

Usefulness: A

Um, yeah, definitely.

Huggability: A

He gets an A for huggability, if you can catch him.

Upgraded by the editors to an **A++** *because HE IS A HERO AND HE SAVED HIS OWNER'S LIFE. Pudding has an amazing story: On the day Amy brought him home, she had a diabetic seizure in her sleep. Sensing her distress, Pudding pounced on her chest to wake her, then ran to her son Ethan's room and woke him up so they could call for help. Best. Cat. Ever.*

grade: **A++**

Mindy

Owner: Ella

Appearance: A

Mindy is gag-inducingly precious. She is small and sleek and has a cutesy-wootsy widdle milk mustache. It makes me want to smack her.

Sociability: A

Mindy is social. Too social. Other cats want to kill her within minutes of meeting her.

Usefulness: F

I would give Mindy a negative usefulness rating if I could. Her presence in the household is actually counterproductive.

Huggability: B

The cool thing about Mindy is that you can pretty much do whatever you want to her, including hugging. She is indifferent.

grade: B−

Rocket

Owners: Ashley and Kim

Usefulness: A

Personal home bug catcher, Rocket has honed her talents to catching flies in midair. She's saved the day from giant house centipedes multiple times.

Huggability: A

The biggest cuddlebug of any cat I've ever known, she bares her belly for lots of rubbin' (and doesn't attack you for doing so).

grade: A−

Kerouac

Owner: Annemarie

Appearance: A

Kerouac is orange and moderately fluffy, with a long tail that looks like a feather. He has a very small face and large ears, giving the impression of an elf.

Usefulness: A

Kerouac likes to crawl into shirts and under covers, providing personal warmth on those cold nights. He is also nice to look at, doesn't destroy the furniture, and is really funny when he jumps into bags.

grade: A

Ollie

Owners: Jordan and Sara

Huggability: A

We have conditioned Ollie to be cuddly to the point of ridiculousness. He enjoys being held for long amounts of time every day, when he will bury his head in your shoulder and begin to snore in a display not unlike cradling a drowsy senior citizen. Every single article of clothing I own looks like a mohair sweater because he just lies on me and rolls around like a meth addict trying to scratch imaginary bug bites.

grade: A

Lyla

Owner: Kelly

Appearance: A

Cutest cat (maybe) ever. I never get sick of staring at her, even when she's an absolute nuisance.

Sociability: B

Lyla is always down to cuddle with human Mommy and Daddy. Maybe a little too clingy.

Huggability: D

Lyla is not a hugger. She is a cuddler. She squirms and looks uncomfortable during any attempted hug or arm restraint, but her otherwise constant, unprompted cuddles make you forget all about the scars obtained from a hug attempt.

grade: B—

Kingston

Owner: Nicole

Appearance: A

The smoldering eyes, the sexy smirk, the fluffy belly hair that goes on for miles—this is what Ryan Gosling would look like covered in luxurious fur.

Sociability: C

Kingston loves Nicole. He's kind of a jerk to everyone else.

Usefulness: B

He evenly distributes handsomeness throughout the apartment, adding not only visual appeal but also monetary value to the property.

Huggability: A

He'll snuggle with Nicole for hours. But if you're not Nicole, he's not interested.

grade: **B+**

Scout and Henry

Owners: Matt and Lara

Cute!

Sociability: A

Immediately upon seeing you—almost regardless of anything else she is doing—Scout will clamber up your body until she is on your chest. Henry's thing is that he plays fetch for bottle caps and paper clips. They both love all people indiscriminately.

Huggability: A

In all our years of having and being around cats, Scout and Henry are among the most huggable we have ever experienced.

Way to go!

grade: A+

Oscar

Owner: Laine

Usefulness: B

Oscar makes me happy. I would consider that a useful attribute. He has a very intense schedule that is split between chewing on the sides of plastic bags and cardboard boxes, licking his own belly, and sleeping.

Huggability: A

Will let anyone pick him up. Will let anyone pet him anywhere. Will sell his soul for a good belly rub. If you get that sweet spot, he doesn't care if it's a serial killer who has broken into the apartment to pet him—just make sure to get a little bit more to the right…right there. Yep.

grade: A−

-THE BAD-

What is it that motivates cats? Aside from basic animal instinct, like eating and sleeping and staying, you know, alive. Well, if the cats in this section are any indication, it's absolute evil. Seriously, cats are monsters. Their sole motivation seems to be doing everything they can to make our lives miserable, and they are really good at it. It's like they're perfectly equipped to make us suffer.

They've got teeth, and they've got claws, and they're not afraid to use either of them. Also, their claws are literally coated in bacteria, because cats are filthy, so even the smallest scratch itches like crazy. They're walking biological weapons with bad attitudes, and we let them live in our homes. What do we expect to happen?

Imagine inviting people over. They come in, pee in your shoes, lick their crotch in front of you, eat any food you leave out, throw up, act surly, and swipe at you anytime you get near them. You'd probably stop being friends with these people. Unless you're into that sort of thing. As it turns out, you are. We all are. We're cat owners, and we're gluttons for pain and punishment.

And the thing is, after all that, they still expect you to feed them and care for them at the end of the day. That's seriously nefarious.

Irwin Chance

Owner: Summer Anne

Sociability: D

Irwin is devoted, kind, loyal, and affectionate—toward me. If a single other person enters the house, he can sometimes be coaxed to prance around the living room to be patted, but that's about it. A few times, I tried to let another cat hang out in our house, but Irwin just hovered over him creepily, and the other cat was obviously really uncomfortable and weirded out.

Usefulness: D

Irwin has no appreciable skills or talents that have any use, although he does come when called and sit on command. But I didn't give him an F because he improves my mood greatly and that's pretty useful.

grade: D+

Bogey Lee
Owner: Amanda

Sociability: D

Bo is not a people person. He will hiss, growl, and smack people he doesn't like, most often strange men in the house. He adores the parents of his human, however, and will purr happily when held by either parent.

Huggability: D

Often when he is snuggly, it's a trap.

grade: D-

Tinhoso

Owner: Lucas

Sociability: B

He likes people. Whenever I have guests over, he comes to greet them and play with them. But he doesn't like his cousin Boo very much, and he's always teasing and biting her.

Usefulness: D

Because of his tendency to annoy Boo, I always have to separate them, and during this time Tinhoso can inevitably be found sleeping in front of the keyboard, farting, and hitting a bunch of keys.

grade: C-

Crash

Owner: Lindsay

Sociability: C

Crash demands attention, which is perfectly normal for a cat, but she doesn't like strangers at all, which is perverse in the extreme.

Usefulness: D

Very annoying while trying to do homework.

Huggability: F

Hates being picked up or hugged but defiantly wants to be petted.

grade: D+

Upgraded by the editors because of her haunting eyes. We don't care if you're a little evil, Crash. We have fallen under your spell! (Only to the tune of an incremental grade change, but still.)

Riley

Owner: Emily

Sociability: C

A devout hater of bags (plastic or paper), the vacuum, and medicine, Riley is usually scampering away from something that just puts him off. Very, very skittish with bags.

Usefulness: D

Litter everywhere and a shredded armchair clearly demonstrate that we are Riley's house staff. He's darn lucky he's cute!

grade: C

BAG

Sweetie

Owner: Liz

Usefulness: D

Sweetie acts like an alarm clock. Sometimes that's not good, like on Saturdays when she wakes me up at 6 a.m. She pushes open doors and opens drawers. Sometimes she gets trapped behind giant armoires or in slotted chairs.

Huggability: D

Sweetie loves being petted but will accept no contact from any stranger. Sometimes I pick her up and hold her upside-down like a baby, and she gives me a death stare.

grade: D−

cat

Dante

Owners: Kyle and Sara

Appearance: A

Dante's fat. He also has a single white ring on his tail. I'd say he's pretty cute overall.

Sociability: F

He's a loner. Prefers to nap by himself wherever he can be alone. Often looks bitter if you try to interact with him and he didn't initiate it. Only openly interacts with people if they have food.

Usefulness: F

Lazy and demanding, he screams at you if a quarter of his bowl is empty until you top it off with fresh food. Always finding new ways to force you into uncomfortable positions in bed. Has a tendency to wake you several hours before your alarm to get more food.

Huggability: A

You can't stay mad at him very long. He looks at you with his huge eyes and fat face, and you just want to squish him.

grade: C

Elly

Owner: Rave

Appearance: A

Even allowing for an owner's partiality, Elly is an empirically gorgeous cat. Her wee nose and paw pads are Disney pink, she has smoky-green Clara Bow eyes, and her fur is of a pleasing autumnal-neutral palette. And she knows it.

Sociability: F

Elly is fearful in the extreme. She tolerates her owner, but almost all other humans and animals are anathema to her. If faced with them, she disappears into another dimension.

Usefulness: D

Elly has three talents: Wookie noises, gnawing through food bags, and being chased around the apartment at 4 a.m. by ghosts. None of these are useful.

grade: C-

Winston

Owner: Patricia

Huggability: D

Winston isn't very huggable. He jumps from being really happy to hissing and meowing when you pick him up and back to happy and playful the moment you put him down. I am the only one in the house who can get him to sit on my lap, and even that only yields a few minutes of comfort before he starts planning his escape.

grade: D

Jasmine

Owner: Kim

Sociability: D

Jasmine rarely desires companionship unless it's to inquire about getting more food. She could probably exist without any interaction with any living being at all, as long as there was some sort of benevolent force in the universe that kept her fed.

Huggability: D

I hug her all day long (I can't help it—she's that cute), but she usually protests by meowing. She doesn't physically try to escape, so maybe she's just playing hard to get. Jasmine is probably the most hugged cat in existence, but she hates every single hug.

grade: **D**

Food

Ender

Owner: Colette

Appearance: B

Ender is large and in charge. He is also all white with some gray spots. He weighs in at eighteen pounds, and people often say, "Wow, what a huge cat!" when they meet him. He also has a very grumpy looking expression at all times. I don't actually ever know when he is happy because he only makes one face, which looks like this: T___T

Sociability: D

Ender could socialize but prefers not to. His main activities are sitting on a chair in my living room, crying loudly to go outside on the front porch so he can go in the garden and guard a tree root that he seems to have grown fond of, or lounging on my roommate's bed in a patch of sunlight and glaring at anyone who tries to pet him.

Huggability: D

Hugging Ender usually results in him squirming in the opposite direction and sometimes moaning. He also hates being kissed and will curl his lips away from his teeth if I try.

grade: C-

Lucy

Owners: Lindsay and Jonathan

Usefulness: C

Lucy doesn't bring any useful skill sets to the table, though she keeps a wary eye on any flies who find their way into the house, and she loves to climb up in the rafters and keep watch for intruders.

Huggability: D

If I were to pick up Lucy and give her a hug, she would be very upset with me. Generally, any squeezes at any time are met with defeated, sad cat noises. Likewise, all of our dog's attempts to snuggle Lucy are met with hisses and swats. It's her way or the highway!

grade: C-

XRAY

Owner: Nikki

Sociability: C

He's social. He likes everybody. He likes other cats, but he will chase cats (and humans) that don't want to be chased, he'll bite you, and he'll attack you if you play my-hand-is-a-mouse. He totally does it out of love though—I hope.

Usefulness: D

I rate him higher than an F because he'll usually greet me at the door, which is worth something.

Huggability: C

He's my teenage son that doesn't want affection from his mother, but I force it on him anyway.

grade: C

Oro

Owner: Rachel

Appearance: B

Oro has very long whiskers, a black nose, big ears, and full cheeks that frame a cute, judgmental glare.

Sociability: C

She likes people who feed her. Everyone else can go to hell. Often watches you eat and makes you feel bad. Jealously despises any girlfriend I have, to the point of growling just in response to her presence.

Usefulness: D

This feline is very good at knocking things off tables, waking you up in the night, and catching nothing. Mostly used for entertainment purposes and foot warming.

Huggability: B

She used to try to make us talk to the paw, but now she has lost her will to fight and passively permits myself and parents to smother her with love. Her tolerance increases as we continue to break her will.

grade: C

Story

(aka Fattyfatty)

Owner: Olivia

Sociability: F

Story doesn't like to be picked up whatsoever. She's a chorus of meows the second her paws leave the floor. She's mildly timid in large crowds and likes one of our cats but not the other. Sometimes I won't see her for days! But I get pillow cuddles almost every night.

Usefulness: F

She loves sleeping. And sleeping. Maybe a little more sleeping. Wait! She also loves to sleep. Maybe that's why she's fat.

Huggability: D

She does this thing where she will stand up on her hind paws by stretching up onto my leg and meow for pets. But the moment I put my hand down to pet her she moves away like, "What?! Are you crazy? I hate cuddles." She's a weirdo.

grade: **D**

Minnie

Owner: Sam

Appearance: B

She's OK-looking for a really old cat. She may be a little crusty around the edges these days, but she has the sweetest face and the cutest wee legs.

Sociability: C

Poor Minnie is terrorized by the neighborhood cats. Because of this, she's too scared to go outside at night and instead stays inside and generates large amounts of meow noise.

Usefulness: F

She poops in the bathroom every day.

Huggability: B

She can be really snuggly when she wants to be. Sometimes she pretends to be snuggly but then runs away.

grade: C-

Flynn

Owner: Holly

Sociability: F

Flynn basically hates everyone and everything but me. He'll attack anyone who comes near him unless they have food. He's very food oriented. He hates my two dogs and doesn't hesitate to give them a what-for, even though they're both large breeds.

grade: **F**

Food

Pogo
(aka Phody & Podiqua)

Owner: Kevin

Sociability: C

Mood swings between absolute fawning and horrific toe biting. Strangers need not apply, or else risk slashes to the face. If you are on the short list of best friends, then you can expect fifteen minutes of snuggly love before the restlessness leads to an inevitable hissy fit. Will destroy personal possessions to stop the use of a cell phone or personal projects.

Huggability: F

Will resist all hugs and snuggles—said embraces must be initiated by Pogo the cat. In the event you do grab the wretch, expect wriggling and jumping and accidental clawing. When in the mood, she will climb onto owner's chest or belly and poke him with painful feet until forced to lie down, where she will remain for fifteen to twenty minutes until she has had her fill, before moving to sit by his feet. Feet are also good for hugging but will eventually be bitten. DO NOT ATTEMPT TO SNUGGLE IN A BLANKET. This induces phobia and, like the vacuum cleaner, must be avoided at all costs.

grade: C-

Juliet

Owner: Chelsey

Sociability: D

Juliet is very jealous of her mama's time. Therefore, she has a hard time socializing with others, especially when they are distracting Mama. She is not a fan of any of Mama's relationships.

Usefulness: C

What she brings to the table in terms of spider catching, sick-Mama cuddling, foot warming, and cuteness, she detracts from in terms of art-supply eating, project ruining, glass smashing, and arm-grabbing bunny kicks. It works out to be pretty even.

grade: C

Jerome Bettis Percible 2.0
(aka The Bus)
Owner: Angela

Appearance: B

The Bus is a good-looking older guy with the portly physique of a post-retirement running back who indulges in too much BBQ and beer. Four years ago, the Woodforest Charitable Foundation crowned him "One of the World's Cutest Pets." He has the certificate hanging above his food bowl to prove it.

Sociability: F

The Bus is not a socialite. He basically hates everyone except me—cats, dogs, people. The Bus does not discriminate. He will attack anyone who enters the house. He especially hates babies and pit bulls.

Usefulness: D

The Bus has a strong preference for drinking water straight from the bathtub faucet. He doesn't seem to care that leaving the faucet running wastes water and drives up the water bill. He is not an environmentalist.

grade: D-

Faile

Owner: Darlene

Appearance: A

Faile has unique markings, to say the least. I call her the Great White Shark.

Sociability: C

Faile is always out and about when people come to visit. She sniffs everything they own and are wearing, then sniffs them again. But she hates other cats. She hisses, growls, and overall acts big and bad. Summary: She loves humans. She dislikes cats.

Huggability: F

Faile absolutely despises being lifted off the ground or being cuddled on the floor. She'll complain with her nagging meows (really, she's the mother-in-law of cats: nag, nag, nag, nag, nag, nag, nag) and try to squirm free. If I capture her in a cuddle on the couch or in bed, she meows as though I've offended her personal right to personal space and darts away as soon as she has the opportunity.

grade: C+

Meow. Meow. Meow.

Jonathan

Owners: Nora and Patty

Sociability: C

This one's complicated. Jonathan loves houseguests who are people! But he deeply hates other cats.

Usefulness: A

It is really useful that we can bring him with us when we go away for the weekend—he very clearly even likes exploring new houses. He did unfortunately recently learn how to vomit in the car.

Huggability: B

On his own terms, dude.

grade: **C+**

Prime Minister Pickles

Owner: Ryan

Sociability: C

If he likes you, he is a sweetheart. If he doesn't like you or doesn't know you, if you pet somewhere that is not one of the approved places (that is, anywhere besides his head or neck), if you carry anything bigger than a pencil case, or if you move faster than he would like, he will hiss and run away. But if he likes you and none of these things occur, he is a very sweet boy!

Usefulness: F

Pickles is a philosopher. He thinks deep, thoughtful things. He thinks them from the bed. Or the couch. Or his condo. But really, besides the deep and thoughtful things, he doesn't do anything else.

Huggability: F

You don't hug Pickles. Pickles chooses when you will be honored to receive his attention. Usually an acceptable time is 3 a.m.

grade: D+

Kombucha

Owner: Hannah

Sociability: D

One of the things I call Kombucha is "weird cat," because that is what she is. She takes a very long time to warm up to people, and once she's fully warmed, she still does not want to be picked up, petted, held, or placed on one's lap. She does consent to sit next to people while they work though.

Huggability: D

Attempting to hug the 'Buch is like hugging a furry rock. Not fun, but also not violent.

grade: C+

Trevor

Owner: Ben

Appearance: A

He needs to be this attractive to balance what a thundering jerk he is.

Sociability: D

Trevor's heart is pitch black. Occasionally, he will get bored and lure you into play before attacking you for having the temerity to touch him. He's happiest on his own, plotting murders.

Huggability: D

Trevor will only tolerate hugging for a maximum of thirty seconds, and there had better be food immediately afterward, because otherwise, boy, are you in trouble.

grade: D

-THE REALLY BAD-

Why settle for a boring old goodie-two-shoes cat or even a petty-criminal "bad boy" cat, when there's a whole dark world of evil masterminds out there to bring color and excitement to your dull life? You'll know one when you see one because the evil comes straight up from the soul and resides in the eyes—those murderous, villainous, piercing eyes that watch you in the dark; that seek out unsuspecting and wholly innocent victims to torment; that unearth trouble in all the darkest places; that remain ever vigilant for new places to vomit up a hairball or two at really just the most inconvenient times, like when you are having a dinner party or something.

Surely that's the kind of cat you want in your life—a Really Bad Cat: a cat with a plan and a personality. A cat with purpose, with vision, with a mission and a motive, with true charisma and a healthy love for chaos with a capital C. None of these milquetoast kitty cats with their purring and sweetness for you—you want some substance and some style in your life. You can handle it. Or can you?

Even the best of cats have days when they forget that it is impolite to scratch the neighbors and unjust to eat the other cat's dinner, but a truly bad cat would never bother himself with such trivial, mundane ways of acting out. A really bad cat bides his time. A really bad cat pretends to be a good boy while his thoughts turn to darker matters. A really bad cat plots his revenge.

Here are some cats who will haunt your nightmares.

Colonel Meow

Owner: Master...but only to her face

Appearance: A

I may appear shifty and shady as hell, but I'm not. I just want that can of tuna you're holding. And your allegiance.

Sociability: A

I use social networking sites all the time. And I think I seem pretty fair.

Usefulness: A

I gave Chuck Norris his balls back, can pour my own glass of scotch, and know how to make Martha Stewart's bundt cake. It was for my grandmother. She hates bundt cake.

Huggability: A

Being vulnerable makes you a man. So thank Christ I'm a cat. Touch me and you die. (The rumors of me liking Snuggies are false…unless I'm loaded. Then proceed.)

grade: *Out of your league*

When the revolution comes, Colonel Meow will be the last thing you see before you're bundled off into a work camp in Siberia for your crimes against the state. Be very, very afraid, because Colonel Meow is the future—and it's not going to be pretty. Even though there will be more Snuggies in it, which is nice.

Mischa

Owner: Julie

Appearance: B

Mischa is very attractive when she tries, though she is a bit of a scruff bag. She cares not if she has the odd dead slug entwined in her locks.

Sociability: F

Mischa is very aloof. She is very suspicious of her sister, Alex. She will occasionally become sociable and lap sit for a few hours but we do not know her reasons for this: we suspect evil thoughts. She greets most visitors with a death stare.

Usefulness: A

Mischa is very useful, especially if you were planning genocide or World War III. She can jump great heights and open closed doors. She is incredibly intelligent. And we suspect most of the time she is plotting world domination, or perhaps doing calculus.

Huggability: F

Mischa does not especially like being picked up, viewing such actions as an attempt to get her in the cat carrier to go to the vet or cattery. However, we have a glimmer of hope—the cattery owner thought she was "more sociable" this time! She must be planning something!

grade: D+

Mr. Licorice

Owner: James

Sociability: F

Social? Wow. No. Mr. Licorice is OK with me, but scared of everything else—everything! This ranges from adorable to utterly frustrating. I have had friends for years who don't believe that I have a cat because he hides from them so thoroughly. I have often shown them that if they look under the bed with a flashlight, they can in fact see the back left corner of what appears to be a cat. Fun times. If he is brought out into company, he is more like a sociopathic carpet than a mammal: utterly immobile and solely focused on the task of hurting or maiming any and all concerned. Other animals? Forget it.

grade: (F)

Lola

Owner: Harrie

Appearance: B

Lola is quite the looker with her long tabby hair—her tail makes her quite the showgirl. She has a smile that makes her look a bit like Salvador Dalí.

Usefulness: F

She's a bit of a liability, smearing poo on the floor, being sick, and molting everywhere. She does tend to get poo stuck in her fur too, and to trim the lumps out, you have to distract her so she doesn't get upset. Also, where we don't have carpet in the flat, you can often see her skidding all over the place when she's doing one of her emergency exits—it can be fairly hazardous avoiding a sliding cat.

grade: D−

meow.

Crookshanks Butter Ball

Owner: Elisabeth

Sociability: F

Honestly, she has no social ability whatsoever, poor fat thing. Occasionally, in the dark of night, she will climb onto us and hum. But then we wake in the morning, thinking we've dreamed the whole thing. Haven't we?

Usefulness: D

Not sure the term *useful* could ever apply to any cat anywhere. If there's any utility at all to Crookshanks, it is that her belly of jelly is a fond reminder of Santa Claus.

Huggability: D

She HATES being hugged, but she is oh so huggable, with her pudding abdomen and her soft white bib. We just have to grab 'er and squeeze.

grade: D

Amelia
(aka Red, Creamsicle, Piggy)
Owner: Alyssa

Usefulness: D

Hardly useful. She spends her days shedding and destroying plants by eating them or peeing on them. Sometimes, she eats too quickly and yaks all over my rug. She also provides great comic relief, as she doesn't actually meow. There's a reason I call her Piggy.

Huggability: F

Every time I pick her up, she squeals, cries, and protests. She will sit next to me and let me pet her hair and brush her for quite a while, but the moment I pick her up, she freaks out and tries to squirm away.

grade:

Isabelle (Iz)

Owner: Sean

Appearance: ~~A~~ F

Appearance mark downgraded by the editors as a result of difficulty in proving this cat exists.

Iz is arguably one of the most austerely beautiful felines in the world. The problem is that proof of her existence can be confirmed only by her owner, who insists that said cat does exist and that she is just hiding at the moment—I swear! Friends feeding the cat refer to it as "feeding the owner's imagination." If you get a glimpse of this rare beast, enjoy its beauty for a fleeting second. Because like the mighty unicorn or the chimera, there is no proof that it exists.

Sociability: F−

If you have a corner or space greater than a quarter inch available in your apartment or house, there is a guaranteed chance that Iz has managed to squeeze herself in there to spend the entire day. She once ran into the rafters of the attic for a week, and it took a professional trapper to extricate her from this new favorite hiding spot.

Huggability: F−

You can't hug air.

grade: F−

Iz has the distinction of having the lowest grade ever given to a cat, which is quite an achievement. We would congratulate her on it if we could only figure out where she is hiding.

Scratch Fury
(Destroyer of Worlds)

Owner: Becky

Appearance: D

Scratch could be said to be a very attractive cat, if it were not for the fact that he is a complete sociopath.

Sociability: F

Scratch will certainly pay attention to you, at your own peril. I know that vets and scientists say that cats forget experiences thirty minutes later and blah, blah, blah, but Scratch is a cat that holds a grudge. Are you sitting the wrong way on the bed? Claws. Not fast enough with that wet food? Claws. Innocent friend trying to keep you alive while your owner is away? Claws. Just all part and parcel of his unique personality.

Huggability: F

Yeah, no.

grade: D-

Annie

Owner: Lousie

Appearance: A

Named after the ginger orphan, because she is one, Annie looks hot most of the time. When excited, she looks like a shark on Ritalin.

Sociability: C

- Known humans = OK
- Cats = bad
- Frogs = good
- Ducks = good
- Strangers = OHMYGODOHMYGOD AMAZING I LOVE YOU PLEASE LOVE ME…

She's not amazing in social situations. Once she pooped in the sink of a house we were staying at for the weekend.

Usefulness: F

Useful? As like what, a doorstop? Once she licked up milk that I spilled.

Huggability: D

I tried to hug her and got a massive bite on my face. Cue a thirty-minute Internet search on the effects of cat bites and the rabies prevalence rate in the United Kingdom. (FYI—only really found in bats, so always use protection.)

grade: D

Barnacles
(aka Jerkface)
Owner: Gustavo

Usefulness: D

In many ways, Barnacles is like a tiny terrorist, and his owners are the oppressive state. This tiny revolutionary starts his day at 5 a.m, demanding food for himself and his oppressed feline brethren. We don't normally negotiate with terrorists, but when he escalates his campaign by knocking small things off of nightstands and dressers and turning on the radio (I am not kidding), we have no choice but to acquiesce to his demands.

Food

grade: D

Meow. Meow. Meow.

Black Kitty

Owner: Emily

Appearance: A

Pretty chill. Likes her stylish coat of black because it transitions seamlessly from daytime catnip binges to afternoon *EastEnders* watching and nighttime soirees. Her coat is also pretty slimming, which is nice.

Usefulness: D

Her frequent gifts of dead or mauled rodents are welcomed in some social circles, but unfortunately not all.

grade: C

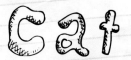

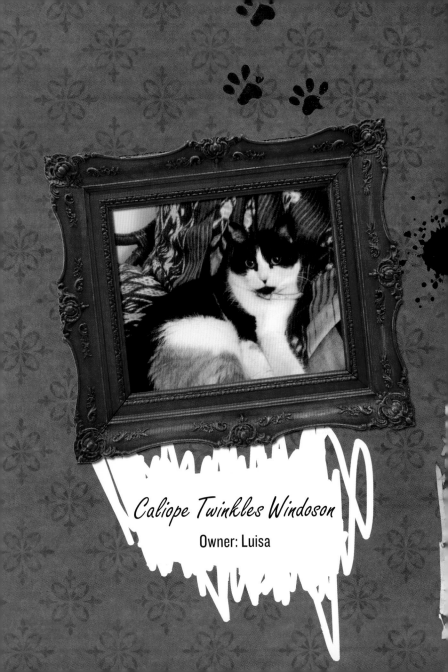

Caliope Twinkles Windoson

Owner: Luisa

Usefulness: A

Caliope does greet visitors at the door, but then she slaps them in the head when they descend the stairs to leave. She can also box. (Watch out for the left hook; she has claws.)

Huggability: F

"Don't touch me." When Twinka wants love, she comes looking for it. Otherwise, please leave her alone, thank you very much.

grade:

Lulu

Owner: Meg

Appearance: B

She's like a pumpkin with legs and a stumpy tail.

Sociability: D

Now that she's solidly middle aged, she comes out to lie around, give everybody the side eye, and eventually pee on the carpet in front of company so that we might all know her displeasure. She loves me, likes my husband, barely tolerates our kid, and wishes everyone else would die in a fire while she watches and laughs.

Usefulness: F

Occasionally, she will kill a bug but then eat only part of it. Her favorite is to leave five or six spider legs behind.

Huggability: F

She would rather die than be held. She also wants to sleep on my head at night.

grade: D-

Lola

Owner: Diana

Usefulness: F

Lola enjoys shredding furniture and pooping on records. She has excellent hunting skills but prefers to practice the catch and release method with cockroaches. Lola has also been known to make a mess (and laugh about it) just for fun.

Huggability: C

You don't hug Lola. She hugs you (like glue).

grade: C−

Mono Blanco

Owner: Lindsay

Sociability: D

Mono Blanco started life as a street kitty on the tough streets of Korea Town, Los Angeles. He's still learning to loosen up and enjoys spending time under the couch.

Usefulness: F

I'm going to go ahead and say that Mono Blanco is not useful. He is not helpful in greeting guests or entertaining, he generally cannot capture string toys but runs at and then past them.

Huggability: F

Oh, he's huggable. As long as you happen to like your hugs with bloody, red streaks down your arms.

grade: D−

Newman

Owner: Jennifer

Usefulness: F

Newman is utterly useless. Period.

Sociability: F

Newman is terrified of anything and everything. He hides from new people, new products, new noises, and new smells. He once ate a hole in the bottom of my box spring and tunneled up there to escape the pressures of his universe. I had to cut him out with a pair of scissors.

grade: F

Pique
Owner: Morgan

Sociability: D

Piqué doesn't like people—at all. Sometimes she will chase a laser pointer, and that is as fun as she gets.

Usefulness: B

She tends to eat the mice, ants, and spiders around the house, so that's really nice of her. She also keeps the squirrels off the bird feeder by making a clicking noise that sounds a lot like Predator.

Huggability: F

Hates people and being touched, but on the off chance that you've wrangled her, she tends to give pretty good hugs.

grade: D+

Zoe

Owner: Emily

Sociability: D

Hates everyone except her owner and sometimes her owner's husband and daughter. Sometimes is nice to people that are allergic to her. Likes the neighbor's dog.

Usefulness: C

Occasionally brings up socks from the laundry room, though sock cleanliness is debatable. Growls when someone is at the door. Brings her favorite stuffed toy to her owners every night without fail.

Huggability: F

Don't even bother. Sometimes she'll sit on your lap, which ends up as a twisted hostage situation where you will get attacked if you move.

grade: **D**

Antonia

Owner: James

Sociability: D

Antonia, about 95 percent of the time, would vastly prefer that no other living being be anywhere within touching distance of her. The only reason she does not get a failing grade here is that during the other 5 percent of the time, when some spirit moves her briefly, she has a startlingly aggressive interactive comportment in which she seems to want you to hold still while she strikes at you repeatedly, all the while looking vaguely ashamed about it.

Usefulness: F

She was discovered in the wild, so for a few weeks after coming home, I suppose she could be forgiven for scarfing her food down at an alarming pace and then puking half of it back up unchewed. It has been five years. She flings litter out of the box with incredible strength and skill that makes a joke of any human innovation to prevent it. She can sense a latent cosmic arrangement of forces that indicates that she is to be brushed and will dematerialize instantly.

Huggability: D

Although Antonia's softness is a draw and she mews adorably, she hates being hugged and sort of goes limp in your arms during an attempt, which is somehow even worse than fighting. And then when it becomes too awkward and you release her, you are left with a small pony's worth of that goddamned orange hair on you.

grade: D

Margarida

Owner: Brad

Sociability: C

Over time, she has become more affectionate and visits once a day to demand almost limitless petting, often lifting her front paw off the ground to meet the petting hand sooner. She does hiss sometimes when we move too quickly, but the hissing has become more obligatory to remind us that she is hard and from the streets.

Usefulness: D

She is moderately useful to us as a daily interaction, but all cats are generally pretty useless in the task orientation sense, so one that lives outdoors and who shows up once a day has to be probably even less useful.

Huggability: F

She is an outdoor cat. Hugging her would mean temporarily trapping her, which means she has been captured by a predator. Not a good idea. She is not a huggable cat. She does not want to be picked up or shut in the house, either. She will freak out. Although she does allow limited back and belly rubs, which is more than you can ask for from some indoor cats.

grade: D

-THE UGLY-

Beauty is in the eye of the beholder and true love sees no imperfections (and all those other things that people say), but when your cat has cross-eyes and half a tail and an overbite that makes her look like a mentally deficient vampire, it's very difficult to love her for her looks.

But contrary to popular belief, cuteness isn't the only thing cats have to offer: They can also bring you nice presents (such as dead mice), help you break in your new furniture, test your reflexes for you by suddenly appearing where you're about to step—lots of stuff.

Some cats, however, are too ugly to love and frankly have very little else to offer at all—but it is one of the great mysteries of the universe that, for some reason, we love them anyway. Indeed, those of us who are blessed with them love these cats more than if they had been some perfect specimen of catliness, born to grace the covers of cat fashion magazines and make inane, vapid comments about world peace at cat beauty pageants.

In many ways, an ugly cat is the best cat of all, a fast friend who will always be waiting for you when you come home from work, waiting to gaze at you adoringly with her cross-eyes, to flash you with that familiar snaggletoothed smile of greeting, to raise that mangled half tail in the air in salute like a flagpole—a sight that is invariably so profound and moving and powerful that you will soon forgive the fact that she has also vomited on your rug and peed in your laundry basket while you were away. How could you stay mad at a face like that?

Here are a few beauties who fit that description.

Kyle

Owners: Grant and Jen

good job!

Appearance: A

Kyle is very precious. Unfortunately, his previous owner removed all his claws and he is unable to scratch himself. This leaves him with a small (read: large) dandruff problem and some greasy fur. An infection in his mouth also mandated the removal of all his bottom teeth but his receding gum line does not deter him from attempting to look his best every day. The extra pounds sit well on his delicate frame, and his permanently crooked ear gives him that exotic look.

Usefulness: A

Kyle provides comic relief both day and night simply by existing.

way to go!

grade:

A+

Kristofferson Quincy
Campbell-Burton

Owner: Summer

Appearance: C

Kristofferson has a limitless capacity for handsomeness, but he's still working on reaching his full potential. I found him on my stoop in the aftermath of a blizzard, and he's all fur and bones right now. His little shoulders stick out at an awkward angle, and his lack of paunch makes him look a little like a leggy supermodel. But that face! Rrawrrr.

Huggability: F

When one is trying to hug Kristofferson, he will kick his legs wildly, squirm like a bored kid at school, and eventually leap from your arms and onto any nearby surface. He is also notably unsquishy, and therefore not that much fun to hug anyway.

grade: D

Lucky Lou

Owner: Meg

Appearance: A

Clearly, Lucky's tough to look at. He thinks that putting on a bunch of fancy stripes will hide his age (he's at the ripe age of sixteen), but he's not fooling anyone. Reality check, Lucky: sunbathing in the window every day ain't doing much for those wrinkles or your snaggle claw. How about spending more time landscaping those paws there, pal? We can hear you approaching from a mile away with that dangly claw.

Sociability: F

If hissing at you when you walk in the door from a long day at work is social, then Lucky is the Vanderbilt of the feline world. Most friends think he's a myth because he disappears into thin air whenever they come over. But then they realize he's very real when he takes a dump right when we're serving dinner.

Usefulness: D

He mostly destroys my rugs with his territorial demeanor. He has been known to catch flies, mice, roaches, and one time a moth the size of a small bird. I have watched him completely gross out over a silverfish though. I guess everyone has their limits.

Huggability: A

This is tough. I give him an A because he hugs me like a person. He will wrap his arms around my neck, and it might be because he is trying to choke me, but I'll pretend it's because he loves me.

grade: C

Sully

Owner: Rachel

Appearance: C

Sully has short white hair. It looks OK, but it's really dry and brittle. If you so much as look at him the wrong way, he sheds. I can't believe he's not bald yet at the rate he sheds.

Sully eats constantly, yet he never gains any weight. He feels like a sack of bones.

Sociability: D

Sully has a very narcissistic personality, and he thinks he's a princess. He absolutely hates everyone and our other kitten. I find that he tolerates me, though. He is always silently judging you. You are in his way; he is not in your way. You better listen to everything he says.

grade: C

Thor

Owner: Jess

Appearance: F

Excessively unphotogenic but slightly more cute in person, Thor is essentially a largish mass of black fur. He is missing part of one ear and has a BB embedded in his face, so in terms of ruggedness, he has some kind of appeal. Maybe. His personality is cute, anyway...Somewhat chubby, with webbed toes, he has a tiny, kittenlike voice that is very much at odds with his otherwise piratelike appearance.

Usefulness: C

He satisfies the requirement of doing cute things that make me happy, but he is fairly useless otherwise. He is extremely messy and doesn't know how to do taxes. He is also possibly one of the dumbest (if sweetest and funniest) cats I have known.

Huggability: A

I am not saying he is the world's most huggable cat, but if there were a contest for that, he would probably place pretty high. I can fall asleep on the couch with him and he won't get up until I do, purring the entire time while I hug him like a teddy bear. Somebody should tell him that cats really shouldn't be like this.

grade: C+

Kitty
(aka the Dark Lord)

Owner: Justyna

Appearance: C

At seventeen, the Dark Lord has lost a bit of her original luster, along with several prominent teeth (including a fang). Her coat is still smooth, shiny, and great for petting—aside from the perpetually crusty tail. With age comes unfortunate issues like dipping your tail in poop and not realizing it. The body is still firm, stubby, and weight has remained a solid seven and a half or eight pounds for many years.

grade: C

cat

Batman Dubstep Everdeen
(aka Batty)

Owner: Sally

Appearance: C

Using conventional standards of cat beauty, Batty is by no means a standout. His ears are a bit big for his head (hence the name Batman), but they suit his larger-than-life personality. He's also really, really fat, but only in the belly and hips. His head and chest don't match the fat tummy that swings around when he walks. He's pear-shaped!

Usefulness: B

He's kind of messy and loves to use the litter box right before we have company. He can sense when a guest is coming over; it's uncanny. But he's so good at making everyone feel better with his cat hugs and kisses, so I'd say he makes a positive impact on the whole.

grade:

B—

Fangsy

Owner: Jennifer

Appearance: C

The fluffy face, his cottony-soft fur, the saucer-sized blue eyes, the look of wonder—all stellar. However, I think we all know why Fangsy has been downgraded to a C. Most of his features scream "high society," except his underbite, which screams "Appalachia." While many people—myself included—find his unique look endearing, it also earned him his moniker. So there's that.

grade: C

Jason

Owner: A.P.

Appearance: F

In his heyday, Jason was the James freakin' Dean of cats. He had hair so smooth and silky—a coat of blackest black and purest white and green eyes so bright they would make your heart hurt. But alas, age did not meet him gracefully. Now, an old fart at eighteen human years, Jason's hair is matted all over, like, Rasta status. One of his eyes is completely clouded over, and he sees as well as, well, Stevie Wonder. Also, he falls a lot, usually unprovoked.

Sociability: F

Jason is a hazard. During those rare moments when he is silent, he is standing right behind you, waiting silently, stealthily for you to turn around and trip over him. He can't laugh (he can't do anything really), but I bet he is on the inside. He regularly craps right next to the litter box, he eats food and then barfs it up, and he sleeps in the middle of the stairs. He is an evil little jerk.

grade: F

Jonah

Owner: Sarah

Appearance: D

Jonah could almost be cute, if he had a soul. His eyes are like looking into the fiery pits of hell. He is borderline obese, which is his only saving grace, as fat cats are typically much cuter.

Sociability: F

Jonah loves attention but hates people. It's a confusing concept, and I'm not sure he even understands how to deal with it. He dislikes almost 100 percent of people but will continuously pester them for attention. Psycho.

Usefulness: F

Jonah is the laziest. He is usually sleeping when he is not terrorizing the house. He takes his food out of the dish before he eats it, making the largest mess. He sheds everywhere and hurts me more than he helps me make friends. Ugh.

grade: D-

Lando

Owner: Rich

Appearance: C

Looks like a cat, only odder. Prominent fangs and hugely oversized ears have led to him being mistaken for a space bat. As a kitten, his head and feet were adult sized. Unfortunately, his body wasn't. He does have a lovely pink nose and very expressive eyes though.

grade: C

Snack Cake

Owner: Emmi

Appearance: F

Snack Cake is a scrofulous cat. Her fur comes out in flaky chunks and as she lurches spastically across a room, her matted hide seems to undulate like a vortex. Snack Cake is approximately 150 years old, which accounts for 60 percent of her inability to clean herself. The other 40 percent is attributable to pure spite, which appears to be her only sustaining element considering the fact that all of her food is immediately regurgitated onto a thing you care about.

Usefulness: D

Snack Cake, while of limited utility, does occasionally justify her existence by providing conversational lubricant for awkward situations. Often, visitors have found themselves baffled when confronted by the stark realities of our home. "Is that a cat?" they ask. "In a manner of speaking," we reply, gently. "It's a matter of some conjecture." Snack Cake will also poop in your luggage, which is of debatable advantage, according to your perspective. I mention this in the interest of parity.

grade: D-

Princess Cuteyface

Owner: Jack

Appearance: D

When I first got my cat, Princess Cuteyface, she was very svelte and had a very cute nose, which was essentially why I agreed to take her in. Unfortunately, cats cannot (at the time of this writing) be sued for breach of contract, because she has since ballooned to a behemoth nineteen pounds as a result of nonstop comfort eating and willful refusal to exercise. I have not given her an F in this category because she does still have a very cute nose.

Sociability: F

Here is a list of individuals my cat doesn't get along with very well:

- Dogs
- Human beings
- Rabbits
- Most plants
- Other cats

Usefulness: C

My cat is essentially a large, angry bed ornament with a cute nose. There are worse things, I guess.

Huggability: B

Princess Cuteyface does enjoy sitting on my lap, which is a very huggable thing to do and should be an important part of any healthy cat-human relationship, so I will give her high marks in this category, even if the experience is akin to having a sack of cinderblocks dumped on your knees.

grade: D

Figaro

Owner: Allison

Appearance: D

My roommate mentioned there was a cat we could adopt from her friend. She said she couldn't look at him the first month she spent time at their house because he was so unattractive. He doesn't receive the worst grade because he has a nice long coat that when not matted looks lovely. And you get used to his face.

grade: D

Cielito

Owner: Audrey

Appearance: C

Cielito's conventionally handsome face is overshadowed by his vile personality. Cielito is overweight, but he doesn't care. He doesn't need your superficial comments about his appearance. If Cielito were a human, he would be the type of man you see on public transportation with long, oily hair, a tiny soul patch, and an ankle-length leather trench coat.

Sociability: F

A true sociopath, Cielito knows exactly how to manipulate you to get what he wants. He chooses his moments of kindness judiciously.

Usefulness: F

Cielito does not have time to be useful because he is plotting the demise of his arch nemesis, the Inflatable Exercise Ball.

Huggability: F

Cielito doesn't know what makes you think that it's okay to hug him.

grade:

F+

Phineus

Owner: James

Appearance: C

Phineus has been called handsome on several occasions—and by handsome, I mean Teddy Roosevelt chomping on some game and looking robust in a national park that he just formed handsome, not John Hamm handsome.

Phineus is big boned with some extra paunch and occasionally some distinctly unattractive dandruff in his plain gray coat, but he does have a distinguished face and is usually smart enough to sit in such a way that his best aspects are most prominent.

grade: C

Bull

Owner: Tanner

Appearance: C

Bull has so much promise—soft white fur, big black eyes, a somber and noble face—but he ruins it all with fatness. I don't think he's capable of licking his own butt, and his overall grooming leaves a lot to be desired. His teeth are rotten—his breath stinks, and he's down to two canines.

Usefulness: F

Bull is anti-useful. He gets food everywhere near his bowl and drops kibble in his water (to soften it up for rotten-toothed chewing), so his water bowl gets gross quickly, too. If his litter box isn't entirely up to snuff—and it never is, because he poops ALL THE TIME— he'll turn any clothing left lying around into his toilet.

Huggability: B

He's a little hard to get a grip on—the best way to carry him is with your arms under his middle and his legs hanging straight down. But when you're in bed, Bull is full of creative ways to snuggle. He'll nest between your legs; he'll spoon you or be spooned. But best of all, he'll come nestle in the crook of your arm and read your book or iPhone over your shoulder.

grade: C

Charlemagne

Owner: Debbie

Appearance: D

Not a looker. He's got a weirdly shaped face with strange white lines running from his mouth to his chin. His right ear is torn and decorated with an interior, odd black splotch. He's also fat.

Sociability: B

He loves other cats, but they hate him because he believes the most sincere expression of love is to bite and scratch. He loves dogs, who also hate him for the same reason the cats hate him. He loves people, who mostly like him, except when he bites and scratches.

Huggability: C

He takes moods. Sometimes he likes it, but sometimes he'll bite and scratch.

grade: C

Dusty

Owner: Amelia

Appearance: F

Quite possibly the ugliest cat ever to knock things off tables and massacre unsuspecting families of sparrows. No whiskers, chunks out of both huge, batlike ears, disproportionate large yellow eyes. Tabby with short, wavy, patchy fur characteristic of his Devon Rex heritage. Also overweight. Has only one facial expression—angry.

Sociability: C

Will slay intruders on sight, be they human, feline, canine, or other. Desperately loyal to his family, to the point of sleeping on their chests and licking their faces at night. Likes to poke peoples' eyes and faces with his paws and meow loudly when they stop petting him. Tends to terrify visiting friends and relatives.

grade: (D)

-THE USELESS-

Let's be honest: All cats are useless. Some are just more useless than others. In fairness, being bad at your job (even when the only nominal responsibility in your job description is occasionally sitting on someone's lap in between naps) requires a pretty special individual. It requires someone who's willing to take it to the next level, to embrace uselessness not as an unfortunate accident of nature, but as an art form, an avocation, a way of life.

If you are a cat and you're thinking about making a career in uselessness, think about these daunting facts before you commit: you will need to be lazier than all the other cats. That means upping your napping time past the eighteen-hour-a-day mark, finding new and creative ways to fall short at unbelievably simple tasks like recognizing your own name or remembering where the litter box is, regularly forgetting who you are or where you live, or even what you do and don't like, and more—so much more. By which I mean so much less. Paradoxically (and this is the last and most valuable piece of advice I will leave you with), when it comes to uselessness, more is less.

OK, so that made no sense, but a truly useless cat wouldn't have bothered to read this in the first place, so it probably doesn't matter. What I am saying is that in Cat World, uselessness is the status quo, and standing out above the crowd—actually distinguishing yourself for uselessness—demands recognition and respect, and it requires a lifetime of dedication to the task.

Here are some of the amazing animals who have proved themselves to be up to the challenge.

Topher

Owner: Chris and Sara

Appearance: A

Topher is big, orange, and fluffy. All the girls want him and the guys want to be him.

Sociability: A

Topher is the life of the party. Once he made a kitten laugh so hard milk came out its nose.

Usefulness: F

Topher likes to help us look good by covering all our clothes in orange fur right before we leave the house.

Huggability: A

Hugging Topher is like hugging a fluffy cloud that bites.

grade: B

Topher is actually Internet famous because of this picture. He walked outside and decided to climb a tree, but was hypnotized by the sudden siren call of a very similar tree two feet away from the one he was climbing...and the rest was history. His thoughtful owners were eventually able to extricate him from his predicament, but not before taking this soon-to-be legendary photograph of their beautiful, brainless boy.

Monroe

Owner: Nicole

Appearance: B

Aside from being slightly cross-eyed, she's downright adorable. And check out that birthmark she shares with her Hollywood namesake.

Sociability: A

The cat's a total slut. She loves me, you, the neighbor, the mailman, the douchebag who just sideswiped my car, the bag boy at the grocery store, the crack addict trying to break into the house…

Usefulness: C

She'd probably help the crack addict carry the TV down the street. That makes her not all that useful to Nicole. The crack addict, however, would find her to be incredibly helpful.

Huggability: A

She can't get enough. Every day is Hug Me Day on Monroe's calendar. When no one else is around, she hugs herself.

grade: (B)

Rio

Owner: Randi

Usefulness: C

I think Rio thinks of cuddling as undignified, but she will curl up on my chest for warmth anytime I am lying down and softly rumble, which has comforted me during sad times for years. Usually during this time she sneezes in my mouth.

grade: **B**

She gets a solid B from me but would probably get an F from anyone else.

Rosie
(aka Potato Cat)

Owner: Julia

Usefulness: D

Rosie has the best of intentions. She regularly does a neighborhood-watch shift from our balcony. She'll chase and eat any bug that's around. I once caught her trying to lure a herd of birds to the window, I assume to kill them, or negotiate their relocation, so she takes home security pretty seriously. She does have this weird biting thing where she'll catch something, like a toy or something, and though she has it in her paws, she'll bite to the left or the right of the object. I don't know what it's all about, but it definitely reduces her effectiveness.

grade: D

Clementine

Owners: Matt and Lara

Appearance: B

Clementine is a real cutie. Her classic black and white markings convey a sense of timelessness and her Marilyn Monroe beauty mark draws stares from every tomcat on the block. To people and cats alike, she's a real looker!

Sociability: A

Clementine is the life of every party. She rolls over to allow people to rub her belly—the more vigorously the better—and she showboats in front of crowds for attention. During a party or gathering, she will be found cruising from lap to lap, standing on tables to be rubbed and coddled. She is a grade-A mingler.

Usefulness: D

For all of Clementine's great qualities, she is not very useful. She doesn't really pull her weight around the house at all, she expects to be waited on hand and paw, and she is standoffish and rude to our kittens. Who could be rude to a kitten? Clementine, that's who. Not useful at all.

grade: B—

Howdy

Owner: Christine

Usefulness: C

She lies on my computer keyboard when I try to work and pulls on my hair when I try to sleep. But her charming confusion and lack of grace and social cues makes me laugh. So that counts for something.

Huggability: D

Sadly, Howdy grew up in a bad home and was pitifully neglected until she was rescued and I adopted her. While six years of love and care have made her sweet and fabulous, she still is quite the flailing songbird when anyone tries to force her into a hug.

grade: (C+)

Fuzzy Joe Biden

Owner: Tiffany

Usefulness: D

Unlike her namesake, Fuzzy Joe Biden is of little use to anyone. If you need someone to knock over your trash bin or claw up your curtains, she is your cat. If you want your food eaten off the table while you go to the bathroom, she is an expert. She is the Apple Genius of clawing holes in your jeans. She will, however, keep your face warm while you are trying to sleep and/or breathe, and she will meow loudly (and constantly) whenever anyone walks by our door in the apartment building.

She's also pretty dumb, running into things on a regular basis and lying on the top of her freestanding scratch post and scratching it from above.

Huggability: D

Will make dying cat noises if you try to hug her.

grade: D

Sebastian

Owner: Lindsey

Usefulness: F

Our other cat always catches mice and bugs and does all the typical cat activities. But when Sebastian finds a mouse or a bug, he just stares at it and does a mixture of meowing and cackling. He gets all excited, but he doesn't know what to do after that.

Huggability: A

He's so huggable that he demands to be picked up when I get home. He meows at my feet until I pick him up. When I do, he climbs onto my shoulders and either stands there and looks at the ceiling as we walk around the house, or he lies there around my neck and sleeps. He loves it.

grade:

Murphy

Owner: Paige

Usefulness: F

I considered rating him somewhat useful for the occasional bug kill that has happened over the years, but because of the number of items he has actually destroyed in my house, I have to rate him not useful. In fact, I'd rate him negative useful if that were an option.

Sociability: D

Despite his handsome outward appearance, inside he is a cold-hearted, vindictive bastard. If his needs are not immediately met, he meows as loud and as often as possible. He then moves on to hiding around corners and leaping out to bite my calves. When guests are over, he will generally either brood under my bed or attempt to snatch whatever food is available. One time he went so far as stealing a cupcake straight from a friend's hands. The second he obtains any food he scampers away growling.

grade: D

Lorca

Owner: Kacey

Usefulness: F

Once there was a cockroach in our house, and Lorca hid in the space between my bed and the wall, quaking in fear. I doubt that he's big enough to kill any rodents, and even if he were, he'd probably just roll his eyes at them and go back to sleep.

Sociability: D

A friend once described Lorca as being "elegantly bored, like a model." Basically, he is above socialization and prefers to sit in a comfortable place and judge other beings. He quietly tolerates humans and cats but can't really be bothered to play with or talk to them. His apathetic attitude coupled with his witchy appearance have led my roommate and I to conclude that he is a goth.

grade: D

Bailey

Owner: Aimee

Usefulness: F

Nothing Bailey does is helpful. Want to clean the litter tray? Bailey will attack the bag full of poo so that poo goes everywhere. Then he takes a poo in the just cleaned litter tray EVERY TIME. Want to sit and watch a film? Bailey will distract you by climbing up you and sucking your hair. Want to have a quiet dinner? Bailey will find multiple routes to climb on the table. Want to put your shoes on? Bailey will play with your laces.

grade: F

meow.

Billy

Owner: Anthony

Usefulness: F

He manages to get in fights, despite never really leaving the house. Birds dive-bomb him, and he is not stealthy or dexterous enough to catch anything but a skinks' tail. He shreds furniture and rugs right in front of you. He also gets underneath couches on his back and claws his way around like a kid on monkey bars, then he hides in the hole he just made in the lining.

Even though he won't let you pet him or even touch him, he will jump up next to you and chew on a newspaper you are trying to read, all while pointing his butt squarely in your face.

He won't eat fresh, healthy human-quality food, only one or two varieties of expensive cat food. He once pulled out a slice of ham from my sandwich, but didn't eat it; he just looked at it for a minute, then walked away.

grade: (F)

Rowdy James
Owner: Patti

Appearance: C

Mr. James is a fat, gray tabby. The word roly-poly comes to mind when describing him. While he has tried Weight Watchers and Jenny Craig and even Nutrisystem, the diet plan he enjoys most is 9 Lives dry food mixed with Friskies Wet Paté. He is known to cheat, however, and sneaks bites of food from Mom's plate when he thinks no one is watching.

Usefulness: F

As Mr. James is completely dependent on his mother for the meeting of his needs, this dependency renders him completely useless. However, if you are a sound editor for films and need someone to replicate the sound of a stampede, he's your man. He has also dabbled in optometry and finds the taste of eyelids delectable.

grade: C-

Django
Owner: Halle

Usefulness: F

Django is not useful at all. He spills drinks on the coffee table and carpet when he's not sticking his face in them, tore up a paper lamp from IKEA, ruined my boyfriend's fifty-dollar headphones, stained the fabric of a chair by constantly sneezing all over it, and only sits directly in front of the TV when we're watching it.

He also scratches and cries at the bedroom door every morning at 6:45, even on the days I don't have to work, until I acknowledge his presence. If I go back to bed, he'll continue to scratch at the door until I get up, and then he ignores me for the rest of the day.

grade: (F)

Mr. Peterson

Owner: Kara

Usefulness: F

He is completely, completely useless. While he can help ease a hangover with his cuddliness, he stares at a bug if he sees it, and sometimes even takes a kitty poo outside the litter box.

Sociability: B

Sometimes he can be a little emo and sit in the middle of the floor and stare off into the distance for hours on end.

grade: ⓑ

cute!

Leeroy

"Crybaby"

Jenkins

Owner: Poppy

Usefulness: F

Thus far, his only demonstrated talents are crying for attention and crop dusting. I will give him this: he is a champion crop duster. His performance art pieces, such as climbing the walls (as captured in the photo) also demonstrate his usefulness insofar as he can wrench your attention away from whatever you were working on. In this respect, he might make a good emergency alarm.

grade: F

Desdemona
(aka Mona and Bunny)
Owner: Olivia

Usefulness: F

Desdemona's great at shedding all over the house, but I don't think that counts toward useful points. Um…she's also great at blending into the dark so when I get up in the middle of the night to pee, I get a leg full of claw. Every. Single. Time. Very useful.

Sociability: D

She doesn't usually come out from under the bed until it's dinnertime. (She's a foodie. She once ate an entire hamburger while I wasn't looking.)

grade: D−

Pearl

Owner: Kendra

Usefulness: D

If sleeping all day and whining for fresh water were useful, then Pearl would get top marks. The water must be fresh for her royal highness. If she has had even a few sips of the water in her bowl, then apparently the water is somehow tainted and must be replenished.

Pearl has never really been outside as she was raised as an apartment cat in Brooklyn, New York, and now that she can access the outdoors in Texas, she has no interest in that nutty world where there's nobody to fill her fresh water bowl.

Sociability: F

She does enjoy simple petting on her head, but beware, you must not touch her butt! As Pearl came from the harsh streets of Brooklyn and lived the beginning of her life with a crazy cat lady and something like thirty other cats, she now has strict rules about how one can engage with her hindquarters. She might tease you by sticking those hindquarters in the air, making it appear as if you should stroke that area, but this is a trick, and she will undoubtedly swipe at you for your insolence.

grade: (D+)

Dedalo

Owner: Azzurra

Sociability: C

He's at first scared when he meets new people, but a bit of food will make a big difference. However, he isn't shy at all with the people he lives with; au contraire, he bites and scratches everyone who comes to hand, paw, whatever.

Usefulness: D

Well, he sleeps and eats all day (and night), so he's not more useful than an ornament, I guess. He also tends to be an attraction for young kids, which would be useful if he didn't have a tendency to be scared of children and hide when they want to play with him, so that kind of cancels itself out. He does tend to sleep in the most peculiar ways, which I guess is good for something.

grade: (D)

Krull
(Springsteen Cat)
Owners: Jay and Rachel

Usefulness: F

If I could score this negatively I would have. The humans are useful to Krull, not the other way around. We groom him, feed him, clean up after him. He is a perpetual two-year-old. Not that we mind doing that because he provides a good friend in return. He won't even kill a bug or mouse in the house. He just follows them and watches them until he becomes bored, then walks away.

Huggability: A

He will let us hold him like a baby and lets our four-year-old lie on top of him. He lies in the crook of our arms or the bend of our legs every night.

grade: (B+)

Upgraded to a B+ because of how awesome his song "Catlantic City" is.

Jenkins

Owner: Sarah

Appearance: A

Jenkins is the handsomest cat in all the land. Just look at his goofy little face! Even the vet says ~~he's sexy.~~*

*That is the exact word she used.

Sociability: B

He's a bit afraid of new people and terrified of new cats, but once he gets used to a situation, all he wants to do is play with you and love you and head butt you and, OK, occasionally attack your feet with his razor-sharp claws.

Usefulness: F

He deserves a negative score here, to be honest. He sharpens his claws on the spines of my books, attempts to eat any piece of paper he sees, wakes me up with predawn foot-pouncing-on, believes power cords to be his mortal enemies, and is not above stealing food right off my plate with his filthy little paws. He is a tiny demon. He's lucky he's the cutest cat to ever exist.

Huggability: A

He makes up for being a demon cat with his extreme cuddliness. If I'm sitting on the couch, he will crawl up my chest, head butt me, and settle in for about an hour of purring. The procedure is very similar when I'm going to sleep.

 grade: B—

*Mooka & Tinkerbell
(aka Mookabell)*

**Owners: Cora and Kevin
(aka Korin)**

Usefulness: C

On the rare occasion our apartment finds itself inhabited by an uninvited entomological roommate, Mookabell is collectively delighted to entertain it, or rather have it entertain them. Eventually, they do away with the creature, though only after much bandying about and behavior that could fairly be described as bug torture. And this seems to be a fairly useful feature, certainly more pleasant and cuddly than the surly exterminator who bangs on the door at 8 a.m. every fourth Saturday morning. Other than that, Mookabell is collectively 1000 percent useless, delightfully so.

grade: (C)

Rufus Whitesocks

Owners: Matt and Chrissi

Appearance: A

Rufus is a very handsome cat indeed, and boy does he know it! If there is preening to be done, then everything else waits while he maintains his dashing countenance.

Usefulness: D

At an early age, Rufus revealed a willingness to be trained. In return for a treat, he will sit and hand the treat bearer his paw. However, this crowd pleaser is no trait of obedience or subservience. Oh no, this is nothing more than a cold business deal. Try as we might, we have been unable to train him to make coffee, turn on the hot water, or to go the bakery to fetch the croissants on a Saturday morning.

grade: C

George

Owner: Eric

Usefulness: D

George is an active agent of gravity and spends much of his time moving your belongings from high energy to low energy states. This is wildly annoying—potentially by design—but it feels like it comes from a loving need to communicate with humans about reserving high places exclusively for sitting.

This benevolent instruction extends to the proper use of doors between rooms, which he strongly believes should be ajar at all times—if not removed altogether. I have no doubt that one day he will succeed in eliminating all of the doors, everywhere.

Huggability: B

Even when he's in the depths of existential doubt and anxiety, you can generally mollify him by pushing him into the couch and holding him against you.

grade: (B—)

Samson

Owner: Brett

Sociability: D

Samson is very skittish and nervous around strangers. Once he gets to know you, he is a total sweetheart who purrs nonstop. He purrs when he's happy, sleepy, and even when he's mad.

Usefulness: C

He is in charge of pest control at our house. He catches and eats bugs, except for spiders. Dragonflies are his favorite. Sam is also a very good watch cat—he stands at attention on the fence post in the front yard for hours watching people come and go. The only problem is that if someone actually approaches the house, he runs away.

grade: (C)

Meg

Owner: Jamie